THIS BOOK IS A

Gift

To: _____

From: _____

On the occasion of:_____

Date:_____

THE RISING OF KINGDOM MILLIONAIRES

FROM STEWARDSHIP TO SOVEREIGNTY

ARMSTRONG EZE-PROPHET

Cover and interior designed in Nigeria by Samap Concepts
samapworld2006@yahoo.com

Published by:

McDougal & Associates
www.ThePublishedWord.com

ISBN: 978-1-964665-41-2

Printed on Demand in the U.S., the U.K., Australia, and the U.A.E.
For worldwide distribution

Dedication

To every faithful steward who has labored in obscurity without being noticed and to every believer who dares to rise from the wilderness of lack and from the ashes of hopelessness and financial limitations into the abundance of God's sovereign wealth. This book is for you. I dedicate these pages to the trailblazers, pioneers, and visionaries who will carry the torch of Kingdom wealth into the nations, proving that prosperity is not selfish accumulation, but divine assignment.

May your journey from stewardship to sovereignty be marked with wisdom, courage, and unstoppable faith. And may you have divine oil and empowerment to stand as God's Kingdom millionaires—financiers of revival, architects of transformation, and vessels of glory and reverence, whose legacies shall never be erased in this generation, nor in generations to come.

Acknowledgments

All glory, honor, and dominion belong to the King of Kings, the Source of true riches, who entrusts His stewards with wealth, not for vanity, but for advancing Kingdom destiny on earth. He is the Master Builder who raises Kingdom financiers for His glory and for the fulfillment of divine mandates and prophecies.

With deep gratitude, I bless my family, spiritual mentors, and God-sent destiny helpers. Your prayers, encouragement, and faith have been rivers of strength, carrying me into the flow of this vision. May the Lord reward you richly and enlarge your portion in His Kingdom.

And to you, beloved reader, this is more than a book; it is a prophetic mantle and divine commissioning. You have not come here by accident. You are marked by

Heaven to rise beyond survival and to step into Kingdom sovereignty. You are chosen to be a vessel of wealth transfer, a financier of revival, a catalyst for national transformation.

Receive this acknowledgment as a prophetic decree:

You are part of a global movement ordained to finance the harvest, empower generations, and shift nations. The hand of the Lord is upon you, and your obedience will echo into eternity. May God open unto you His good treasure, cause you to lend to nations, and make you a sign and wonder of Kingdom prosperity. You are called, chosen, and commissioned for such a time as this. Amen!

Contents

Preface

The 21st century has opened a new chapter for the Body of Christ. We are witnessing the unfolding of prophecy, as God is raising up a generation of men and women who will not only preach the message of the Kingdom, but also finance its advance. We are living in a time when stewardship is being tested and sovereignty is being entrusted.

This is not just another book on wealth; it is a prophetic compass for a new breed of Kingdom financiers whom God is raising up in these last days with a divine shift from survival mindset into the authority of sovereignty, from merely managing resources to governing with wealth as Kingdom ambassadors. Far too long the narrative of wealth has been dominated by greed, corruption, and self-indulgence, but God is rewriting the story. He is raising up Kingdom millionaires who see money, not as a master but as a mandate, not as a possession but as a platform; not as an idol, but as an instrument for transformation. As I wrote this timely piece, I felt the undeniable wind of the Spirit stirring me, whispering that the time had come.

Why This Book Matters Now

The nations of the earth are in a time of shaking as economies crumble, systems fail, and currencies lose their strength. Yet, in the midst of this chaos, the covenant of God stands unshakable: *"it is he who gives you the power to get wealth, that he may establish his covenant"* (Deuteronomy 8:18). So, this book is for the dreamers, the builders, the intercessors, and the visionaries who sense a divine call to wealth but refuse to be trapped in greed. It is for those who long to see nations discipled, churches resourced, and the Gospel preached without financial limitation.

You will discover that being a Kingdom millionaire is not about ego or extravagance; it is about covenant, stewardship, and assignment. It is about money with a mission. In this era, God is pouring out an anointing for Kingdom financing like He did in Bible days in the lives of people likes Joseph, Daniel, Esther, and Deborah, men and women who are ready to function as champions and stewards of divine resources and rise into places of influence for the sake of Kingdom advancement. Wealth in their hands is not hoarded; rather it is harnessed to becomes a weapon against poverty, a seed for revival, and a tool for the transformation of nations.

This is a Journey:
From Stewardship to Sovereignty

Every believer begins as a steward—entrusted with little, tested in faithfulness, and proven in integrity. Stewardship is where character is forged and discipline is cultivated. It is the training ground where we learn that *"the earth is the LORD's, and the fullness thereof"* (Psalm 24:1).

But stewardship is not the destination. God's intention is promotion—bringing us into sovereignty, where we do not just manage resources but command influence. Sovereignty is rulership under divine authority. It is walking in the dominion mandate of Genesis 1:28, where wealth and influence are leveraged for the fulfillment of God's purposes in every sphere of life—government, business, education, media, arts, and family.

Sovereignty is not about pride; it is about positioning. It is not about flaunting wealth, but fulfilling destiny.

What You Can Expect

As you turn the pages of this book, prepare for a transformation of your mindset. You will discover:

- The biblical principles that unlock Kingdom wealth.
- The divine laws that shift you from managing pennies to governing millions.
- How to align your financial life with covenant promises.
- The dangers of greed, materialism, and self-centered prosperity.
- The call to rise as a Kingdom financier whose wealth fuels revival, missions, and societal reformation.

A simple reminder: this is not a prosperity manual; it is a Kingdom mandate. The goal is not simply to "get rich," but to be entrusted with divine resources to establish God's covenant in the earth.

If you are ready to dive deep into this timely revelation, make these Kingdom millionaire declarations:

- Today, I rise as a steward proven and a sovereign appointed.
- I declare that I am a Kingdom millionaire in the making, not for vanity but for divine assignment.

- I am a faithful steward of God's resources.
- I will manage well what is placed in my hands, and I will multiply it for the glory of God's Kingdom.
- I am anointed to create, manage, and release wealth.
- Ideas, opportunities, and divine connections flow to me.
- Nations will open their doors to the wisdom and wealth I carry.
- I reject poverty, greed, and financial fear.
- I embrace abundance, generosity, and covenant prosperity.
- I am a channel, not a container.
- I am a financier of revival, a pillar in God's Kingdom economy.
- By the authority of Heaven, I will rise from stewardship to sovereignty, and I will use my wealth to establish God's covenant in the earth.

In Jesus' name, Amen!

A Call to Action

I challenge you, reader, to approach this book, not with casual curiosity, but with holy expectation. Read with your Bible open, your heart surrendered, and your spirit ready to be stretched. Allow the Holy Spirit to renew your thinking and enlarge your vision.

Why? Because you are not just called to make a living; you are called to make a Kingdom impact. You are not just called to survive; you are called to reign. You are not just called to be a steward; you are called to step into sovereignty.

Rise, therefore, as one of God's Kingdom millionaires in this generation. May your life be the proof that God still raises up financial giants to finance His eternal purposes. The journey begins here.

Read this book prayerfully. Let each decree become your confession, each devotional your meditation, and each revelation your launching pad. You are not just reading a book; you are stepping into a movement that will change your life for the better and present you with the golden opportunity to engrave your name in God's Hall of Faith.

Welcome to the making of Kingdom millionaires of our time.

Introduction

Why God Is Raising Up Kingdom Millionaires Now

We are living in prophetic days. Economies are shaking, nations are in turmoil, and systems are collapsing. But, in the midst of this chaos, God is positioning His people for influence.

Why?

- Because the last great revival requires resources. The Gospel is free. Yes, indeed, but the means to spread it to the nations is costly.
- Mission fields need missionaries.
- Media platforms require funding.
- Orphanages must be built.
- Schools, hospitals, and city-wide crusades need financiers.

The world has billionaires funding ideologies of darkness. How much more must God raise up millionaires who will fund righteousness, truth, and revival?

The Scriptures are clear:
"My cities through prosperity shall yet be spread abroad"
(Zechariah 1:17).
"The wealth of the sinner is stored up for the righteous"
(Proverbs 13:22, NKJV).
"The abundance of the sea shall be turned to you"
(Isaiah 60:5, ESV).

This is not prosperity for pleasure; it is prosperity for purpose.

This book will show you the pathway from stewardship to sovereignty, from managing little to ruling over much, from being a consumer to becoming a financial apostle of the end-times. It's time to arise, shine, and embrace your financial mandate. You are called for such a time as this.

Arise, O Kingdom Millionaire!
Beloved, this is your moment. The Spirit of God is brooding over a new breed of men and women who will not bow to mammon, but will rise as mighty financiers of the Kingdom.

Do not say, "I am too small, I have too little, I am too old." Abraham started at 75, Joseph started in prison, and David started in the wilderness. God is not limited by your background; He is only waiting for your surrender.

This is your prophetic hour to step into covenant wealth. The nations are waiting for your obedience. The Gospel is waiting for your investment. Generations yet unborn are waiting for your legacy.

Arise, O Kingdom millionaire! Take your place as an apostle of finance. Fund revival. Build cities. Disciple nations. Leave a legacy that echoes into eternity.

The Lord is saying:
"I will make you a ruler over many, for you have been faithful with little. The silver is Mine, the gold is Mine, and I am putting it into your hands for My glory."

Kingdom Instructions
- Go forth
- Build
- Multiply
- Reign

The making of God's Kingdom millionaires of our time has begun, and you are one of them.

Armstrong Eze-Prophet

PART I

THE CALL TO KINGDOM WEALTH

1

The Rise of Kingdom Millionaires in the Last Days

The world is at a prophetic tipping point. Economies are shaking, systems are collapsing, currencies are failing, and yet, in the midst of this uncertainty, a new generation is rising—Kingdom millionaires.

These are not self-made moguls drunk with greed; they are Spirit-filled believers, men and women handpicked by God, carrying wealth with a mission, prosperity with a purpose, and riches with responsibility.

The Scriptures declare:

"And I will shake all nations, so that the treasures of all nations shall come in, and I will fill this house with glory, says the LORD of hosts. The silver is mine, and the gold is mine, declares the LORD of hosts" (Haggai 2:7-8).

This prophetic shaking is not accidental; it is deliberate. God is redistributing wealth and repositioning it in the hands of those who will not squander it on selfish ambition, but will use it to fund revival, transform societies, and prepare the earth for the coming of the King.

The Prophetic Transfer of Wealth

Throughout history, God has used economic shifts to advance His purposes.

In Egypt, Joseph became the custodian of national wealth, not for himself, but to preserve the nation of Israel (see Genesis 41).

In Babylon, Daniel rose to prominence and influence through divine wisdom, shaping the destiny of kings and kingdoms.

In the early Church, Lydia, a businesswoman dealing in purple, financed the apostolic mission of Paul (see Acts 16:14–15).

Today, that prophetic baton is being passed to a new generation.

The Spirit of God is raising up financial apostles—believers who see money, not as status, but as stewardship.

Why Kingdom Millionaires Now?

We are living in the end-time harvest season. Jesus declared, *"This gospel of the kingdom shall be preached in all the world for a witness unto all nations, and then shall the end come"* (Matthew 24:14).

In Mark 13:10 (KJV), the word used means "to publish among all nations." For the Gospel to be published and reach nations at the scale and speed required, it will demand resources—billions, even trillions. Media, education, technology, humanitarian missions, church planting, and nation-building initiatives all require divine funding.

The days of the Church being financially crippled are over. God is raising up sons and daughters who will finance His agenda with boldness, excellence, and abundance.

Kingdom Millionaires Are Different

Worldly millionaires pursue wealth for selfish reasons. Kingdom millionaires pursue wealth for divine purpose and legacy.

The world's system produces wealth through exploitation, manipulation, and greed. The Kingdom produces wealth through covenant, stewardship, and obedience.

That is why Deuteronomy 8:18 says: *"But thou shalt remember the LORD thy God: for it is he that giveth thee power to get wealth, that he may establish his covenant which he sware unto thy fathers, as it is this day."*

The mark of a Kingdom millionaire is not just how much they have, but how much they release for eternal impact.

A Prophetic Call

This book is a prophetic call to rise into your millionaire mandate, not to boast and not to compete, but to advance the Kingdom of God.

The time has come to shift:

From struggling to surviving, from surviving to thriving, and from thriving to reigning. God is saying to this generation: "I am raising you up from stewardship to sovereignty."

Prophetic Decree:

(Declare this out loud with faith.)

"I am not called to be broke; I'm called to be a blessing. I step into the covenant of wealth. The shaking of nations will not shake me out; it will position me in. I rise as a Kingdom millionaire, a financier of revival, and a custodian of divine resources. In Jesus' name, Amen!"

✢ Kingdom Millionaire Devotional Prayer ✢

Day 1: The Owner of Wealth

Scripture:
"The silver is mine, and the gold is mine, saith the LORD of hosts" (Haggai 2:8).

Meditation:
God is not broke, nor is He limited. The earth and its fullness belong to Him. Kingdom millionaires must first recognize that they are not owners, but stewards. Wealth flows to those who understand divine ownership.

Prayer:
"Father, I acknowledge You as the Source of all wealth. I surrender my finances, skills, and opportunities into Your hands. Make me a faithful steward of Your riches. In Jesus' name, Amen!"

Step into Action:

Write down one financial habit of yours that shows God you trust Him (e.g., tithing, generosity, integrity). Now commit to that habit this week.

2

Every true Kingdom millionaire must understand this foundational truth: wealth in the Kingdom is not accidental; it is covenantal.

Deuteronomy 8:18 declares: *"But thou shalt remember the Lord thy God: for it is he that giveth thee power to get wealth, that he may establish his covenant which he sware unto thy fathers, as it is this day."*

God does not bless randomly; He blesses covenant keepers.

Wealth Is Not about Money; It's about Covenant

The world chases wealth as an end; the Kingdom receives wealth as a means. God's covenant with Abraham, Isaac, and Jacob was not only about land and inheritance; it was about raising up a people who would reveal His glory through abundance.

When you enter a covenant with God, your wealth is not merely for personal comfort. It becomes a divine instrument to advance His purposes.

Three Pillars of the Covenant of Wealth

1. Faith in God as the Source
Genesis 22:14
Jehovah Jireh is the true Provider.

2. Obedience to Kingdom Principles
Malachi 3:10–11
Tithing, giving, generosity, and stewardship.

3. Commitment to Kingdom Assignment
Matthew 6:33
Seeking the Kingdom first ensures that wealth flows with divine backing.

Worldly Riches vs. Covenant Wealth

Worldly riches are temporary, corruptible, and often destructive.

Covenant wealth makes an eternal   impact, leaves a generational   blessing, and creates Kingdom expansion.

Abraham was not just rich in silver and cattle; he was wealthy in legacy.

Joseph's riches were not for display but for preservation. Solomon's prosperity brought nations to Jerusalem to seek God's wisdom.

Your Invitation

God is still looking for men and women who will say: "Lord, if You bless me, I will bless nations. If You prosper me, I will build Your house."

Wealth that is covenantal does not enslave you; it empowers you.

Make a Prophetic Decree with Faith:

"I am a covenant child of God. Wealth is my inheritance, not my struggle. I will not chase money; money will run after me. I receive the power to get wealth and to use it for the glory of God. Amen!"

♖ Kingdom Millionaires Devotional Prayer ♖

Day 2: The Covenant Connection

Scripture:
"Seek first the kingdom of God and his righteousness, and all these things shall be added unto you" (Matthew 6:33).

Meditation:
Kingdom wealth is never about seeking money first; it is about seeking the King first. When your priorities align with Heaven, provision becomes automatic.

Prayer:
"Lord, re-order my desires. Let me hunger for Your Kingdom above riches, and let wealth be added as a tool for Your purposes."

Step into Action:
Identify one way you can prioritize God's Kingdom this week—giving, serving, or investing in souls. Then act it out.

3

Kingdom millionaires are not raised up to live in luxury alone; they are raised up to solve problems. Examples: Matthew 27:57-60 and John 19:38-42.

In the book of Genesis, Joseph's journey reveals the pattern: from the pit to the palace, not for personal fame, but for prophetic purpose.

Joseph: A Model for Kingdom Millionaires

Genesis 41:57 declares: *"And all countries came into Egypt to Joseph for to buy corn; because that the famine was so sore in all lands."*

Joseph was not just a dreamer; he was a divine distributor. God positioned him as a solution to global famine. His wealth was tied to a mission: to preserve life and fulfill prophecy.

The Joseph Mandate

1. **Prophetic Insight:** Joseph received wisdom and dreams that revealed divine economic solutions.
2. **Strategic Stewardship:** He stored up in times of plenty to prepare for the coming famine.
3. **Generational Preservation:** His mission ensured that Israel survived and God's covenant continued.

The Modern Josephs

- Today's Kingdom millionaires are modern Josephs,
- Business leaders funding missions and education,
- Entrepreneurs creating jobs that lift families out of poverty,
- Investors building infrastructure that shapes nations.

The Joseph mandate is about being positioned in the marketplace, not merely for profit, but for prophetic purpose.

What Makes Millionaires with a Mission Mindset Different?

- They ask, "What problem am I solving for the Kingdom?" not "How much can I accumulate?"
- They see wealth as a divine assignment.
- They are unshaken by famine because they have prepared in times of plenty.

A Prophetic Decree

Declare with boldness:

"I carry the Joseph mandate. My wealth will solve problems. My resources will preserve generations. I will not hoard; I will distribute resources to expand God's Kingdom. Nations will be blessed through me. In Jesus' name, Amen!"

✤ Kingdom Millionaires Devotional Prayer ✦

Day 3: Millionaire with a Mission

Scripture:

"You are the light of the world. A city set on a hill cannot be hid" (Matthew 5:14).

Meditation:

Wealth in the Kingdom is not meant to hide you; it's meant to position you as light. Your finances carry a mission to make Jesus visible in the earth realm.

Prayer:

Father, give me a Joseph's kind of heart. Make my prosperity a platform for solution. Position me in this generation as a light-bearer with resources that glorify You.

Step into Action:

List three areas where your finances could be used to solve problems in your community or church. Begin with one of those actions this week.

PART II

THE MAKING OF KINGDOM MILLIONAIRES

4

The Test of Stewardship: Faithful in Little,
Ruler Over Much

Every Kingdom millionaire goes through God's classroom of stewardship before entering sovereignty.

Jesus said:
"He that is faithful in that which is least is faithful also in much. ... And if ye have not been faithful in that which is another man's, who shall give you that which is your own?" (Luke 16:10–12).

Stewardship Is God's First Test

Before God entrusts you with millions, He tests you with hundreds. Before He gives you companies, He tests you with salaries. Before He gives you nations, He tests you with neighbors. If you waste the little, you will also waste the much.

If you are unfaithful with another man's, you disqualify yourself for your own.

Three Realms of Stewardship

1. **Personal Finances:** Budgeting, saving, investing, and avoiding debt.
2. **Opportunities:** How you handle small platforms determines if God will open global doors.
3. **Relationships:** Managing people and resources with integrity attracts divine partnerships.

Financial Habits of Stewards Who Become Millionaires

- They keep good records (see Proverbs 27:23).
- They honor God with their first-fruits (see Proverbs 3:9–10).
- They plan for the future without neglecting generosity, tithing, and their offspring.
- They see money as seed to be planted, not just as spending power.

A Prophetic Decree

Declare with faith:

"I am faithful with little; therefore I will be entrusted with much. I will not waste seed; I will multiply seed. My stewardship qualifies me for sovereignty. In Jesus' name!"

⤴ Kingdom Millionaires Devotional ⤴
Day 4: A Steward of Increase

Scripture:
"Moreover it is required in stewards, that a man be found faithful" (1 Corinthians 4:2).

Meditation:
Faithfulness in secret attracts promotion in the open. Every act of integrity in managing resources is a stepping stone to greater wealth.

Prayer:
"Lord, make me faithful in my stewardship. Train my hands to handle resources wisely. Prepare me for greater responsibility."

Step into Action:
Track your spending for 7 days. Then ask yourself: "Does this reflect good stewardship or waste?"

5

The Spirit of Creativity and Innovation

The Spirit of God is the ultimate wealth-generator. Kingdom millionaires do not just hustle; they receive divine ideas, innovations, and blueprints that propel their creativity, discovery, and productivity

Isaiah 45:3 promises:
"I will give thee the treasures of darkness, and hidden riches of secret places, that thou mayest know that I, the LORD, which call thee by thy name, am the God of Israel."

Creativity: The Currency of Kingdom Wealth

- Joseph received a divine economic strategy that saved nations.
- Daniel received divine wisdom that positioned him in government.
- Bezalel was filled with the Spirit of God for creativity in craftsmanship (see Exodus 31:2-4).

Kingdom millionaires are Spirit-Filled Innovators

They carry Heaven's ideas for earth's problems. They are God's Heaven-to-earth supernatural conduit through which divine ideas flow.

1. **Prayer and Sensitivity: Ideas that produce** wealth are often born in prayer, intercession, and waiting upon God.

2. **Prophetic Insight:** God reveals what is coming before it arrives (see Amos 3:7).

3. **Execution Excellence:** It's not enough to hear; obedience and action are also key.

Why Creativity Is Superior to Capital

Many chase money, but the wealthiest people chase ideas. Capital without creativity dies. Creativity attracts capital. When you bring together people with great ideas, you attract great capital.

Proverbs 8:12 **says:** *"I wisdom dwell with prudence, and find out knowledge of witty inventions."*

A Prophetic Decree

Declare boldly:

"I am filled with the Spirit of wisdom and creativity. I receive divine strategies, witty inventions, and supernatural ideas that will birth wealth for the Kingdom."

੭ Kingdom Millionaires Devotional ੭
Day 5: Wisdom Code for Wealth

Scripture:
"I wisdom dwell with prudence, and find out knowledge of witty inventions" (Proverbs 8:12).

Meditation:
Every invention, innovation, and wealth solution comes from divine wisdom. God's Spirit makes you a carrier of creative solutions.

Prayer:
"Holy Spirit, flood me with creative wisdom. Reveal hidden riches and treasures of darkness to me. Make me a channel of divine innovation."

Step into Action:
Write down 3 business or ministry ideas that have come to you in prayer. Choose one of them to explore this month.

6

The Discipline of Wealth:
From Bread Eaters to Bread Givers

Money has two assignments: bread to eat, and seed to sow. The test of a Kingdom millionaire is learning the discipline to eat some and sow most.

2 Corinthians 9:10 says:
"Now he that ministereth seed to the sower both minister bread for your food, and multiply your seed sown, and increase the fruits of your righteousness."

The Problem with Bread Eaters
- They consume everything they get.
- They live paycheck to paycheck, spending without saving, and have nothing left to sow.
- This lifestyle keeps people in debt, financial slavery, permanent tenanthood, and generational bondage.

The Power of Bread Givers

They understand that:

- Money is a servant, not a master.
- Seed multiplies when sown, but its potentials are trapped when hoarded.
- Discipline is the bridge between wealth and poverty.

The Practical Discipline of Kingdom Millionaires

1. **Budgeting:** Tell money where to go, don't ask where it went.
2. **Saving:** Proverbs 21:20 — *"There is treasure to be desired and oil in the dwelling of the wise."*
3. **Investing:** Money should work while you sleep, not sleep while you work.
4. **Giving:** The highest discipline is generosity. It positions you at the corridors of influence and power.

From Consumer to Distributor

When the boy gave his lunch of five loaves and two fishes, it multiplied to feed thousands of souls, and there was a surplus left over. That is the picture of Kingdom wealth distribution. It creates multiplication, not deduction (see Matthew 14:17-21).

A Prophetic Decree:

Declare with conviction:

"I refuse to be a bread eater only; I am a bread giver. My seed will multiply. My giving will feed millions. I am disciplined in wealth, positioned for abundance, and entrusted with divine resources. In Jesus' name.

֍ Kingdom Millionaires Devotional ֍
Day 6: Prosperity Pathway

Scripture:

"There is treasure to be desired and oil in the dwelling of the wise; but a foolish man spendeth it up" (Proverbs 21:20).

Meditation:

The difference between wisdom and folly is discipline. Wealth require structure, not impulse.

Prayer:

"Lord, deliver me from wastefulness and the spirit behind unrealized wasteful spending, including its ability to lure me, seduce me, and or hold me in an endless circle of captivity year after year. Teach me discipline, budgeting, saving, investing, and giving. Make me a faithful bread giver."

Step into Action:

Set a personal giving goal this month beyond your tithe. Choose one ministry, mission, or need to sow into. Set a savings and investment goal this month for the next six months to one year.

PART III

THE ASSIGNMENT OF KINGDOM MILLIONAIRES

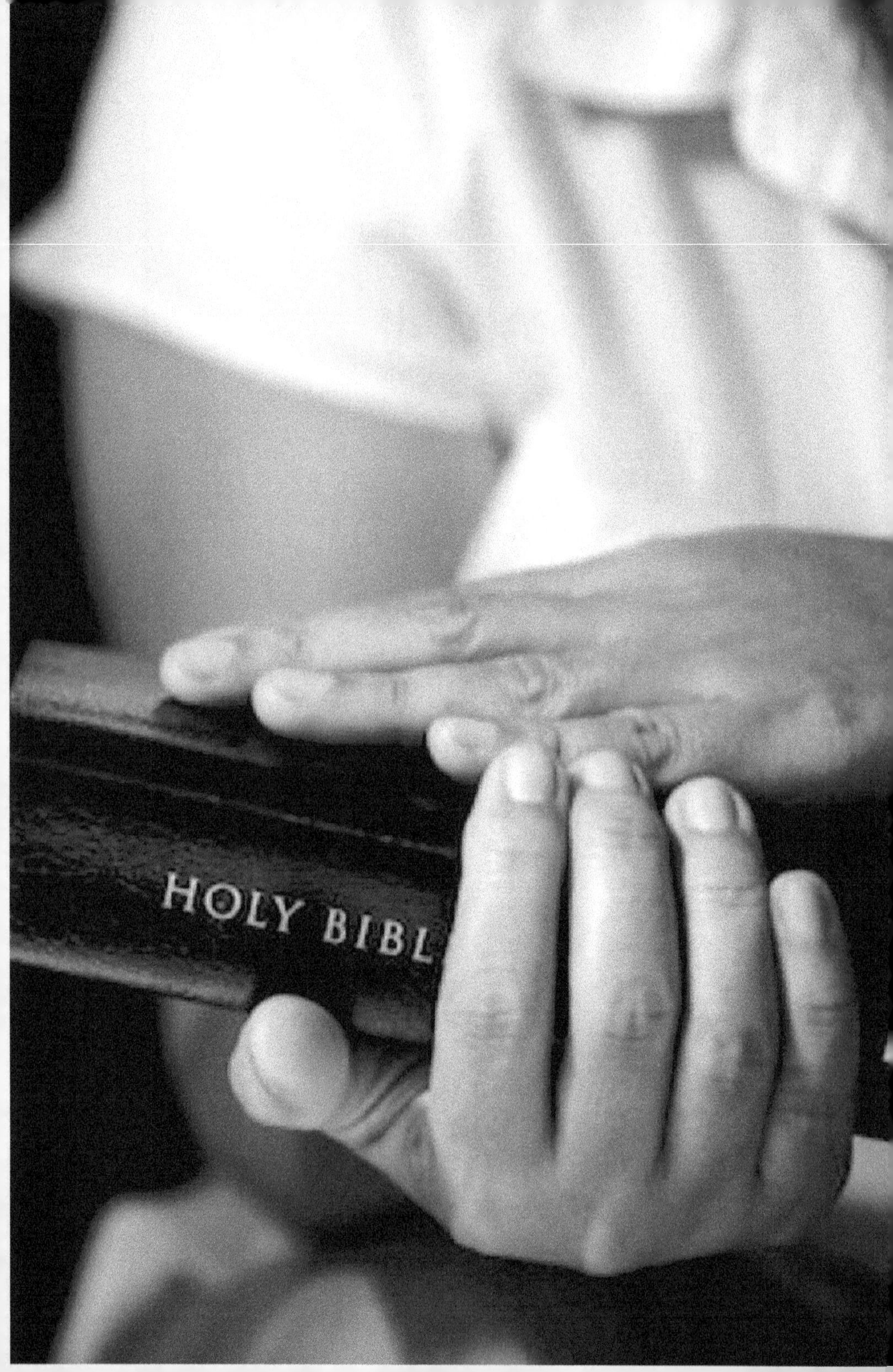
HOLY BIBL

7

The greatest assignment of Kingdom millionaires is to fund the spread of the Gospel.

Romans 10:14-15 says:
"How then shall they call on him in whom they have not believed? ... And how shall they preach, except they be sent?"

Preachers need to be sent, and sending requires resources. Missionaries need travel, churches need land, Gospel media need platforms, schools need funding. None of these move without Kingdom financiers.

The Lydia Example

Acts 16:14-15 introduces Lydia's testimony. She was a wealthy businesswoman dealing in purple cloth. She opened her home to Paul and the other apostles, financing and facilitating the spread of the Gospel without giving in to family grubbing or peer pressure because she understood her calling and the legacy she was determined to build. Today her name remains in biblical archives.

Kingdom millionaires today are modern-day Lydia's strategically positioned to underwrite and sponsor revival.

Why Kingdom Wealth Is Critical for the Gospel

To finance missions and church planting, expanding God's Kingdom on earth, and to keep the Church financially relevant in a changing world.

To Support:
- Media evangelism
- TV Programs
- Radio programs, and
- To keep God's presence in all digital spaces
- To establish Christian education systems
- To fund social impact projects that demonstrate Christ's love
-

Kingdom Wealth = Kingdom Expansion

Every dollar, every naira, every pound, every euro or cedi given into the Kingdom becomes an eternal investment. Unlike worldly riches that fade, Gospel financing places the involved in the chronicles and epistles of the hall of faith, creating a legacy with echoes into eternity.

A Prophetic Decree:
Declare with boldness:
"I am a financier of the Gospel. My resources will preach Christ, plant churches, send missionaries, disciple nations, and add to my credits in glory. My giving will echo in eternity."

⮑ Kingdom Millionaires Devotional ⮐
Day 7: Power to Get Wealth

Scripture:
"Give, and it shall be given unto you; good measure, pressed down, and shaken together, and running over..." (Luke 6:38).

Meditation:
Giving into the Gospel is not loss; it is multiplication. Heaven records every seed sown into souls, and God sees you as partners in the expansion of His Kingdom on earth.

Prayer:
"Father, give me the grace not to give wealth unwarranted reverence as an idol or a monument, but as

a tool for Your Gospel propagation. Position me to finance revival in this generation."

Step into Action:

Make it a point to partner financially with a missionary, an evangelism project, and/or church initiative this month.

8

Today's Kingdom millionaires are not just church builders; they are nation builders, policy makers, philanthropists, and investors.

Proverbs 29:2 says:
"When the righteous are in authority, the people rejoice."

The Kingdom needs leaders who can influence policies, establish businesses, enhance agriculture, and reshape cultures.

Joseph in Egypt

Joseph's financial stewardship preserved nations during famine. He became a nation builder through God-given wisdom.

Daniel in Babylon

Daniel used divine wisdom to counsel kings, influencing the destiny of entire empires. His position carried great economic impact.

Modern Kingdom Millionaires as Nation Builders

Funding hospitals, schools, and humanitarian projects and influencing government policies to align with justice and righteousness.

Using Wealth To:

- Transform communities
- Lift the poor
- Feed the hungry
- Create jobs

From Church Impact to National Impact

The assignment of Kingdom millionaires goes beyond tithing to a local church. God is raising up a generation that will shape national economies and industries.

A Prophetic Decree

Declare with conviction:

"I am called to be a nation builder. My resources will transform communities, influence policies, and shape generations for the glory of God."

૭ **Kingdom Millionaires Devotional** ૭
Day 8: Gatekeepers of Influence

Scripture:
"You are the light of the world. A city that is set on a hill cannot be hid" (Matthew 5:14).

Meditation:
Your wealth is not meant to hide you; it is meant to position you as a city on a hill. Kingdom millionaires shine in governance, business, and social transformation.

Prayer:
"Lord, position me as a light in my nation. Use my resources to transform communities and influence generations."

Step into Action:
Identify one national or community issue—education, healthcare, or poverty—and then ask God how you can contribute toward solving it.

9

Jesus made a profound statement in Luke 16:11:

"If therefore ye have not been faithful in the unrighteous mammon, who will commit to your trust the true riches?"

This reveals a powerful truth: money is not the true riches; it is only the test.

The Purpose of Money

- It is a tool.
- It is temporary.
- It is the least in the Kingdom hierarchy.

But how you handle money determines whether God can entrust you with:

- Spiritual authority
- Eternal impact, and/or
- Greater influence

59

True Riches Defined:
- The souls saved through your giving
- The lives transformed through your generosity
- The generations impacted by your legacy
- The heavenly rewards that cannot be corrupted

Why God Is Careful with Wealth
God does not release financial sovereignty to those who see money as an idol; He releases it to those who see money as a means to an eternal end.

Shifting Perspectives
Kingdom millionaires live with eternity in mind. They know that every investment into the Gospel is stored in Heaven's treasury.

A Prophetic Decree
Decree with faith:
I will not pursue just temporary riches; I will pursue true riches. My money is a tool for eternal impact. My wealth will echo in Heaven.

⤷ Kingdom Millionaires Devotional ⤶
Day 9: The Economy of the Spirit

Scripture:
"Lay up for yourself treasures in heaven, where neither moth nor rust doth corrupt ..." (Matthew 6:20).

Meditation:
Earthly wealth fades; heavenly wealth endures. Every soul touched through your giving is an eternal treasure.

Prayer:
"Father, align my heart to true riches. Teach me to use money as a servant, not as a master. Make my wealth a ladder to eternal reward."

Step into Action:
Make one eternal investment this week by supporting evangelism, discipleship, or a soul-winning ministry.

PART IV

THE PATHWAY TO SOVEREIGNTY

Transformation from ordinary stewardship into rulership, generational influence, and end-time financial apostleship.

10

From Steward to Sovereign: Promotion for Faithfulness

Every Kingdom millionaire begins as a steward, but God's ultimate goal is to make you a sovereign, one who rules with authority in finance and influence.

Jesus said: *"Thou hast have been faithful over a few things, I will make thee ruler over many things: enter into the joy of thy Lord"* (Matthew 25:21).

The Graduation of a Steward
Stewardship = proving faithfulness.
Sovereignty = exercising rulership.

When God finds you trustworthy in little, He gives you ownership, authority, and dominion in much.

Signs of a Sovereign
1. You influence economies, not just households.
2. You release resources with authority.
3. You speak, and systems shift in your favor.

Joseph moved from steward of Potiphar's house to sovereign of Egypt's economy. Daniel moved from slave to sovereign advisor of kings.

Your Inheritance

Sovereignty is not just about money; it is about influence, authority, and legacy. Kingdom sovereigns manage wealth to establish God's will on earth.

A Prophetic Decree

Declare with authority:

"I am rising from stewardship to sovereignty. I will rule with integrity, govern wealth with wisdom, and use my influence for Kingdom expansion."

✣ Kingdom Millionaires Devotional ☙

Day 10: The Overflow Dimension

Scripture:

"The wealth of the sinner is laid up for the just" (Proverbs 13:22).

Meditation:

Sovereignty means stepping into rulership of resources God has prepared for you. You are no longer waiting; you are taking your rightful position.

Prayer:

"Lord, graduate me from stewardship into sovereignty. Entrust me with wealth, influence, and dominion for Your Kingdom."

Step into Action:

Write down three areas in your life where God has tested you with little. Then ask yourself: Am I ready for more?

11

True Kingdom millionaires do not think in years; they think in generations.

Proverbs 13:22 says: *"A good man leaveth an inheritance to his children's children: and the wealth of the sinner is laid up for the just."*

The Principle of Legacy
- The rich think about income.
- The wealthy think about assets.
- The Kingdom millionaire thinks about generations.

Abraham passed blessings to Isaac, Isaac to Jacob, and Jacob to Israel. That's generational wealth with covenant continuity.

How to Build Generational Wealth

1. **Establish Kingdom Values:** Teach your children financial stewardship early.
2. **Diversify Resources:** Invest in assets that will outlive you (land, businesses, systems).
3. **Document Legacy:** Wills, trusts, and foundations preserve Kingdom impact.
4. **Mentor the Next Generation:** Pass on wisdom, not just wealth.

Why Generational Wealth Matters

Money without values breeds corruption, but wealth with covenant values becomes revival across generations.

A Prophetic Decree

Declare with faith:

"My wealth will not die with me. I will leave a legacy of faith, finance, and influence for my children's children. My seed shall possess the gates of nations."

✤ Kingdom Millionaires Devotional ✤

Day 11: A Legacy of Kingdom Wealth

Scripture:

"The just man walketh in his integrity: his children are blessed after him" (Proverbs 20:7).

Meditation:
Generational wealth begins with generational values. Integrity is the true inheritance you leave.

Prayer:
"Father, give me wisdom to build wealth that outlives me. Help me to raise children who will steward riches for Your glory."

Step into Action:
Start writing a legacy plan for how your resources, business, or ministry will outlive you.

12

The End-Time Millionaire Mandate

The climax of this journey is the end-time wealth transfer. The Scriptures have prophesied it, and this generation will see it.

Haggai 2:8-9 says: *"The silver is mine, and the gold is mine, saith the LORD of hosts. The glory of this latter house shall be greater than of the former."*

The Prophecy of Wealth Transfer

Proverbs 13:22 — *"The wealth of the sinner is laid up for the just."*

Isaiah 60:5 — *"The abundance of the sea shall be converted unto thee."*

Zechariah 1:17 — *"My cities through prosperity shall yet be spread abroad."*

God is raising up end-time millionaires as apostles of finance to fund the last great harvest.

Characteristics of End-Time Millionaires

1. **Radical Generosity:** They give without fear.
2. **A Kingdom-First Mentality:** They build altars before they build mansions.
3. **A Global Vision:** They see wealth as a weapon to reach nations.
4. **An Unshakable Faith:** They thrive even in economic crises.

Your Mandate

You are not called just to survive; you are called:

- To fund revival,
- To transform nations, and
- To usher in the coming of the King

A Prophetic Decree

Declare with fire:

"I am an end-time Kingdom millionaire. I am an apostle of finance. My wealth will fund revival, disciple nations, and prepare the earth for the return of Jesus!"

⑂ Kingdom Millionaires Devotional ⑃
Day 12 : The Kingdom Wealth Mandate

Scripture:

"Arise, shine; for thy light is come, and the glory of the LORD is risen upon thee. ... The forces of the Gentiles shall come unto thee" (Isaiah 60:1 and 5).

Meditation:

This is the hour of your rising. You are not called to be hidden; you're called to be a financial light to nations.

Prayer:

"Lord, anoint me powerfully today and make me part of the end-time millionaire mandate. Use me to fund the Gospel, influence nations, and glorify Jesus here on earth."

Step into Action:

Dedicate a percentage of your income exclusively to end-time Gospel work. Treat it as a non-negotiable Kingdom investment.

12 Financial Prayers and Decrees for Kingdom Millionaires
anchored in the Scriptures, prophetic authority,
and covenant revelation

1. A Prayer of Covenant Wealth Based on Deuteronomy 8:18

Father, I thank You for giving me the power to
get wealth to establish Your covenant.

Today, I align my finances with Your Kingdom's
purpose.

I declare that I am a covenant millionaire, raised to
fund revival and impact nations.

2. A Prayer of Divine Ownership Based on the Revelation of Haggai 2:8

Lord, I acknowledge that silver and gold belong
to You.

I am but a steward of Your resources.

I decree: Wealth flows into my hands because
I'll manage it faithfully for the Owner, God
Almighty.

3. A Prayer to Break Poverty Strongholds Based on 2 Corinthians 9:8

From now on, every mindset of lack and limitation is destroyed in my life.

I embrace Kingdom abundance.

I decree: I am free from poverty, lack, and debt. I walk in supernatural provision.

4. A Prayer of Seedtime and Harvest Based on the Authority of Genesis 8:22

Father, I sow in faith, knowing that no seed is ever wasted in Your Kingdom.

I decree a hundredfold harvest over every seed I release for Your Kingdom advancement.

5. A Prayer for Wealth Transfer Based on Proverbs 13:22

Lord, position me for the end-time wealth transfer.

Let resources shift from the wicked into the hands of the righteous.

I decree: Resources are released into my hands to fund God's agenda.

6. A Prayer of Wisdom for Wealth Based on Proverbs 8:18

Father, grant me divine wisdom, strategies, and ideas that will birth lasting wealth.

I decree: I am walking in divine innovation, creativity, and financial insight for generational impact.

7. A Prayer for Favor with Finances Based on Psalm 5:12

Lord, surround me with favor in contracts, opportunities, and partnerships.

I decree financial doors open before me locally and globally without struggle on my part.

8. A Prayer for Financial Multiplication Based on Matthew 14:19-20

Lord, bless the work of my hands and cause increase in all I do.

I decree supernatural multiplication of my resources, businesses, and investments.

9. A Prayer Against Financial Devourers Based on Malachi 3:11

Father, rebuke every devourer, every wasting spirit, and every leakage in my finances.

I decree: My finances are protected, preserved, and fruitful in Jesus' name.

10. A Prayer of Kingdom Assignment Based on Matthew 6:33

Lord, let my wealth always serve Your Kingdom purpose, not selfish ambition.

I decree: My prosperity is an instrument for winning souls, nations, and for Kingdom expansion.

11. A Prayer for Generational Wealth Based on Proverbs 13:22

Father, help me build wealth that will outlive me and continue to bless generations after me.

I decree: Financial legacies are rising through me. My children will never know poverty.

12. A Prayer of Financial Apostleship Based on Isaiah 60:5

Lord, make me a financial apostle, one who carries wealth for Kingdom transformation.

I decree: I am anointed for affluence and ordained to carry wealth with a mission.

10 Laws of Kingdom Wealth

1. The Law of Covenant Alignment

> Deuteronomy 8:18 — *"It is he that giveth thee power to get wealth, that he may establish his covenant."*

- Wealth flows to those aligned with God's covenant.
- Without covenant, prosperity becomes vanity; with covenant, prosperity becomes destiny.

2. The Law of Divine Ownership

> Haggai 2:8 — *"The silver is mine, and the gold is mine, saith the LORD."*

- God is the Owner, and we are but stewards. When you recognize His ownership, you position yourself for trust and greater release.

3. The Law of Faithful Stewardship

> **Matthew 25:21** — *"Well done, thou good and faithful servant: thou hast been faithful over a few things, I will make thee ruler over many things."*

- Millionaires are first made in the stewardship of little things.
- Faithfulness with the small attracts Heaven's promotion.

4. The Law of Seed and Harvest

> **Genesis 8:22** — *"While the earth remaineth, seedtime and harvest ... shall not cease."*

- Giving is not loss, but rather investment.
- The size of the harvest is determined by our faith and obedience in sowing.

5. The Law of Value Creation

> **Proverbs 22:29** — *"Seest thou a man diligent in his business? he shall stand before kings."*

- Kingdom wealth is birthed by solving problems and in excellence and diligence in adding value to lives and communities. This opens doors of influence and resources.

6. The Law of Wisdom and Innovation

Proverbs 8:18—*"Riches and honour are with me; yea, durable riches and righteousness."*

- Ideas from the Spirit create wealth. Millionaires pray for wisdom more than for money because wisdom produces sustainable riches.

7. The Law of Multiplication

Matthew 14:19-20—Jesus blessed the loaves, and they multiplied.

- God's wealth is never stagnant. He blesses what you release and multiplies what you manage with thanksgiving and faith.

8. The Law of Kingdom Assignment

Matthew 6:33—*"Seek ye first the kingdom of God and his righteousness; and all these things shall be added unto you."*

- Provision flows toward assignment.
- When your wealth is tied to God's purpose, you will never lack divine backing.

9. The Law of Generational Transfer

> Proverbs 13:22 — *"A good man leaveth an inheritance to his children's children."*

- Kingdom wealth is not consumed, but preserved and multiplied across generations for legacy impact.

10. The Law of an Abundance Mindset

> 2 Corinthians 9:8 — *"God is able to make all grace abound toward you."*

- Poverty is first broken in the mind. Abundance is a mentality before it is a reality. Think Kingdom, not scarcity, and resources will flow accordingly.

A 30-Day Kingdom Millionaire Devotional

➤DAY 1—The Power to Prosper

- I enter into covenant with wealth on the authority of Deuteronomy 8:18.

➤DAY 2—The Owner of Silver and Gold

> *"The silver is mine, and the gold is mine, saith the* Lord *of hosts"* (Haggai 2:8).

- In line with Haggai 2:8, I covenant with God, the Creator and Owner of everything, to empower me with wisdom and entrust me with wealth, natural and material resources.
- I acknowledge that wealth does not originate with man; it originates with God. He is the true Owner and Source, and by recognizing His ownership, I appropriate the authority to manage His resources with freedom and faith.

My Father, I acknowledge You as the Owner of all wealth. Make me a faithful manager of Your resources.

My Prophetic Declaration: I am not an owner, but a steward. I call forth God's resources to flow through me for Kingdom impact.

➢DAY 3—Breaking the Spirit of Poverty

2 Corinthians 8:9—*"Though he was rich, yet for your sake he became poor, so that ye through his poverty might become rich."*

Meditation: Poverty is not my covenant portion. Jesus paid the full price so that I can live in sufficiency and abundance.

Lord, I renounce every poverty mindset. Fill me now with the faith to walk in Christ's wealth.

My Prophetic Declaration: I walk in abundance because Jesus took my poverty on the cross.

➢DAY 4 —The Abrahamic Blessing

Genesis 12:2—*"I will bless thee ... , and thou shalt be a blessing."*

Meditation: God's blessings upon me is not for luxury alone, but so that I can become a channel of blessing to nations.

Father, release the Abrahamic blessing upon me and make me a blessing to generations.

My Prophetic Declaration: I am blessed to be a blessing. Nations shall drink from my overflow.

➢DAY 5—Faithful Stewardship

Luke 16:10—"He that is faithful in that which is least is faithful also in much."

Meditation: Before God entrusts you with millions, He tests you with hundreds. Be sure to pass the test of stewardship.

Lord, train me to be faithful with little so that I can be entrusted with much.

My Prophetic Declaration: Lord, I am faithful in little; therefore I am qualified for much.

➢DAY 6—The Joseph Principle

Genesis 41:40—"Thou shalt be over my house ...; only in the throne will I be greater than thou."

Meditation: Joseph prospered because he solved problems on a national scale. True wealth comes to problem-solvers.

God, give me divine strategies to solve problems that bring glory to You.

My Prophetic Declaration: Like Joseph, I carry wisdom that nations cannot ignore.

➤DAY 7— Breaking Mammon's Hold

Matthew 6:24—*"Ye cannot serve God and mammon."*

Meditation: Money must be your servant, never your master. Mammon enslaves, but Kingdom wealth empowers.

Lord, deliver me from every hidden worship of money.

My Prophetic Declaration: I serve God, not Mammon. Therefore, wealth serves me for Kingdom purposes.

➤DAY 8—Wealth with a Mission

Acts 4:36-37—"*Barnabas, ... having land, sold it, and brought the money, and laid it at the apostles' feet.*"

Meditation: Kingdom wealth funds Kingdom work. Your wealth is not just for comfort, but for the Gospel's advancement.

Father, make my finances a weapon in the hands of Your Church.

My Prophetic Declaration: My money is my ministry. My wealth is for Kingdom mission.

➤DAY 9—Streams of Income

Genesis 2:10—"*And a river went out of Eden to water the garden; and from thence it was parted, and became into four heads.*"

Meditation: God gave Adam multiple streams in Eden, and Kingdom millionaires build multiple streams of income.

Oh Lord, show me the streams You have ordained for my life.

My Prophetic Declaration: I am flowing in multiple streams of income and Kingdom wealth.

➤DAY 10—The Power of Generosity

Proverbs 11:25—*"The liberal soul shall be made fat: and he that watereth shall be watered also himself."*

Meditation: The more you give, the more you grow. Generosity is the secret of Kingdom millionaires.

Oh Lord, enlarge my heart to give beyond measure.

My Prophetic Declaration: I am a river of generosity. I prosper by refreshing others.

➤DAY 11—Wisdom for Wealth

Proverbs 8:18—*"With me are riches and honor, enduring wealth and prosperity."*

Meditation: True wealth is tied to divine wisdom. Seek wisdom, and riches will come.

Lord, let wisdom guide every financial decision I make.

My Prophetic Declaration: I'm walking in divine wisdom that attracts wealth and honor.

➤DAY 12—Divine Ideas

Isaiah 45:3—"I will give thee the treasures of darkness, and hidden riches of secret places, that thou mayest know that I, the LORD, which call thee by thy name, am the God of Israel."

Meditation: God gives creative, innovative ideas that unlock hidden treasures.

Holy Spirit, inspire me with fresh ideas for wealth creation.

My Prophetic Declaration: I receive hidden treasures and divine abilities for innovations.

➢DAY 13—Excellence as a Key to Wealth

> Daniel 6:3—Daniel so distinguished himself that the king decided to set him over the whole kingdom.

Meditation: Excellence attracts favor, promotion, and wealth, while mediocrity repels them. Excellence is not perfection, an important distinction. It is doing ordinary things with extraordinary grace.

> *Lord, clothe me with the Spirit of excellence. Let my work, my decisions, my conduct, and my stewardship reflect Your glory. Make me distinguished in every sphere of influence.*

My Prophetic Declaration: I declare that an excellent spirit is upon me. I rise above mediocrity. I excel in my business, my assignments, and my calling. By excellence, I attract wealth, honor, and divine opportunities. I am distinguished for greatness.

➢DAY 14—The Anointing for Wealth

> Isaiah 61:6—*"Ye shall be named the Priests of the Lord: ... ye shall eat the riches of the Gentiles."*

Meditation: The Spirit of God empowers us for wealth. Therefore, I declare today, "I have received the anointing for financial dominion."

Lord, anoint me for wealth and influence.

My Prophetic Declaration: I am anointed for Kingdom wealth and global influence.

➤DAY 15—Breaking the Cycle of Financial Delay

Joel 2:25— "I will restore to you the years that the locust hath eaten."

Meditation: My Father breaks every cycle of stagnation and restores all wasted years.

Lord, accelerate my financial destiny and redeem my lost years.

My Prophetic Declaration: I prophesy recovery of all lost time, and I step boldly into accelerated abundance.

➤DAY 16—Kingdom Influence through Wealth

Proverbs 22:29—*"Seest thou a man diligent in his business? he shall stand before kings"*

Meditation: Wealth opens doors to influence and leadership.

Lord, position me to influence kings and leaders with Kingdom values.

My Prophetic Declaration: I am a Kingdom influencer through covenant wealth.

➤DAY 17—Breaking the Bondage of Debt

Proverbs 22:7—*"The borrower is servant to the lender."*

Meditation: I refuse to be in debt because debt is a financial enslaver. As a Kingdom millionaire, I am walking in freedom already.

Father, deliver me from the trap of debt.

My Prophetic Declaration: I am debt-free and I will remain debt free by operating in financial freedom in Jesus' name.

➢Day 18—Righteous as the Foundation of Wealth

Psalm 112:3— *"Wealth and riches shall be in his house: and his righteousness endureth for ever."*

Meditation: Kingdom wealth rests on righteousness, never on greed or corruption.

Lord, purify my motives concerning wealth.

My Prophetic Declaration: My wealth rests on righteousness; therefore it will endure.

➢DAY 19—Funding Revival

Zachariah 1:17— *"My cities through prosperity shall yet be spread abroad."*

Meditation: Prosperity is not for vanity; it is for Kingdom expansion. God funds revival through willing vessels, Kingdom financiers, who carry both the burden and the resources to build for Him. Your wealth is a weapon, and your resources are revival fuel.

Lord, make me a financier of Your move. Let my prosperity advance Your Gospel, build Your Kingdom, and ignite revival in nations. Use me as a channel of divine supply for the end-time harvest.

My Prophetic Declaration: I declare that I am a Kingdom financier, chosen to fund revival. My resources will build God's cities, empower His missionaries, and expand His Gospel. I am a carrier of prosperity that ignites revival.

➢DAY 20—The Multiplication of Grace

Matthew 14:19—*Jesus multiplied the loaves and fishes.*

Meditation: Kingdom wealth is not just addition, but also multiplication.

Lord, breathe multiplication on my resources, so that they go further and bless many more.

My Prophetic Declaration: What I carry multiplies supernaturally in Jesus' name.

96

➢DAY 21—Integrity in Wealth

Proverbs 28:20— *"A faithful man shall abound with blessings."*

Meditation: Integrity is the foundation of enduring wealth.

Oh, Lord, keep me faithful and upright in my dealings.

My Prophetic Declaration: My prosperity comes now with integrity. And let my wealth overflow in Jesus' name.

➢DAY 22—The Power of Vision

Habakkuk 2:2— *"Write the vision, ... make it plain."*

Meditation: Millionaires are visionaries. I receive the ability to write, plan, and pursue the vision God gave me.

My Father, my Maker, sharpen my vision for wealth creation and Kingdom impact in Jesus' name.

My Prophetic Declaration: I am a visionary steward of Kingdom wealth.

➤DAY 23—A Prophetic Wealth Transfer

Proverbs 13:22—" *The wealth of the sinner is laid up for the just.*"

Meditation: In this season, God will shift resources from ungodly hands to Kingdom hands.

Lord, position me for the coming wealth transfer.

My Prophetic Declaration: I am a recipient of God's end-time wealth transfer.

➤DAY 24—Kingdom Partnerships

Ecclesiastes 4:9—*"Two are better than one, because they have a good reward for their labour."*

Meditation: Wealth creation often requires divine partnerships and alliances.

Lord, connect me to destiny partners for Kingdom wealth.

My Prophetic Declaration: I call forth faithful Kingdom partners to come and work with me to advance the Kingdom.

➢DAY 25—Wealth that Speaks Generationally

Psalm 112:2—*"His seed shall be mighty upon the earth."*

Meditation: True Kingdom wealth blesses children and children's children.

Lord, make my wealth speak for generations.

My Prophetic Declaration: My legacy is generational prosperity in and through righteousness.

➢DAY 26—Overcoming the Fear of Risk

Ecclesiastes 11:4—*"He that observeth the wind shall not sow; and he that regardeth the clouds shall not reap.."*

Meditation: Fear blocks wealth. Millionaires move in bold faith.

Lord, give me an anointing for boldness that enables me to take faith-inspired risks.

My Prophetic Declaration: I am bold in faith. I plant in faith and I reap an abundant harvest without hindrance or delay, in Jesus' name.

➤DAY 27—Kingdom Wealth and Nations

Isaiah 60:5—*"The abundance of the sea shall be converted unto thee."*

Meditation: God's plan is for the wealth of nations to flow into His Kingdom.

Oh Lord, let the wealth of nations flow into my hands for Kingdom use.

My Prophetic Declaration: The abundance of nations is released to me now for Kingdom assignment.

➤DAY 28—Prophetic Giving

2 Kings 4:9-10—The Shunamite woman's generosity opened the door to a prophetic miracle.

Meditation: Giving unlocks prophetic doors to abundance.

Lord, lead me into the kind of giving that provokes Heaven's attention to release a quick response and remarkable results in Jesus' name.

My Prophetic Declaration: From today, my giving will activate prophetic blessings and divine abundance.

➤DAY 29—An Eternal Perspective on Wealth

Matthew 6:20—*"Lay up for yourselves treasures in heaven."*

Meditation: Earthly riches fade, but eternal investments last forever.

My Father, align my wealth with eternity.

My Prophetic Declaration: I command my wealth to start building eternal treasures in Heaven.

➤Day 30—Commissioned as a Kingdom Millionaire

Matthew 25:21—*"Well done, thou good and faithful servant: thou hast been faithful over a few things, I will make thee ruler over many things."*

Meditation: The Bible makes it clear that you have been called, equipped, and commissioned as a financial apostle and a Kingdom pillar in this generation.

My Father and my King, I receive my commission as a Kingdom millionaire. I surrender my life and my everything to You. Use me to disciple nations through wealth.

My Prophetic Declaration: I am a financial apostle of God's Kingdom and I rise to fund revival and transform nations in Jesus' name.

How to Contact the Author

Armstrong Eze-Prophet can be contacted directly about his book or for speaking engagements at:

ezeprophetministries@gmail.com

www.ingramcontent.com/pod-product-compliance
Lightning Source LLC
LaVergne TN
LVHW011336080426
835513LV00006B/391